READING TO DIDCOT

Vic Mitchell and Keith Smith

MP Middleton Press

Cover picture: "Saint" class 4-6-0 no. 2936 **Cefntilla Court** runs into Didcot on the down relief line with the 5.8pm all-stations from Reading on 16th August 1947. A light engine stands on the centre siding, which existed until 1974. On the right are the main lines and the single line to Newbury. *(H.C.Casserley)*

Published March 2002

ISBN 1 901706 79 6

© *Middleton Press, 2002*

Design   Deborah Esher
Typesetting   Barbara Mitchell

Published by
            Middleton Press
            Easebourne Lane
            Midhurst, West Sussex
            GU29 9AZ
Tel: 01730 813169
Fax: 01730 812601

Printed & bound by Biddles Ltd,
            Guildford and Kings Lynn

INDEX

ACKNOWLEDGEMENTS

We are very grateful for the help received from many of the photographers mentioned in the credits and also for the assistance received from C.L.Caddy, G.Croughton, J.B.Horne, M.King, N.Langridge, Mr D. & Dr. S.Salter, G.T.V.Stacey, C.Whetmath, E.Youldon and our ever helpful wives, Barbara Mitchell and Janet Smith.

I. Railway Clearing House map from 1947

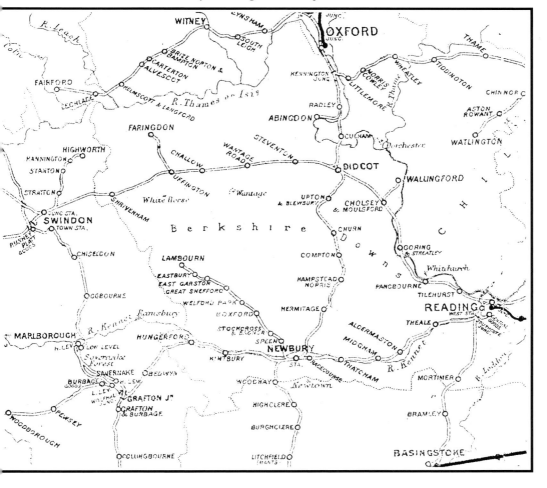

GEOGRAPHICAL SETTING

The route runs close to the River Thames, which forms the boundary between Oxfordshire and West Berkshire to a point north of Goring. The Goring Gap in the Chiltern Hills allowed the track to be laid on fairly level ground, although meanders of the river necessitated some substantial cuttings to minimise curvatures.

The Wallingford branch ran roughly parallel to the Thames, whereas the main line was built on slightly higher ground to give a direct route to Didcot.

Soon after leaving Reading, trains run onto the Chalk of the Chilterns and traverse it for about 12 miles. The western end of the route and the Wallingford branch were constructed mainly on Upper Greensand and Gault Clay.

The maps are at the scale of 25ins to 1 mile, unless indicated otherwise. North is at the top, except where there is an arrow.

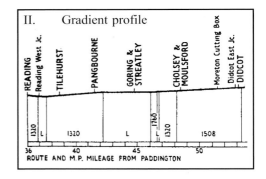

HISTORICAL BACKGROUND

The Great Western Railway reached Reading from London on 3rd March 1840. The engineer was I.K.Brunel and it was constructed under an Act of Parliament dated 31st August 1835.

The line was extended beyond Didcot to Steventon on 1st June 1840, the entire route being built to the broad gauge of 7ft 0¼ins. It reached Bristol on 30th June 1841. A branch from Didcot to Oxford opened on 12th June 1844 and one from Reading to Newbury and Hungerford followed on 21st December 1847.

The broad gauge impeded the flow of goods traffic between the Midlands and the South of England and so a third rail was added between Basingstoke and Oxford, traffic commencing on 22nd December 1857. A similar short link was provided through Reading to connect with the South Eastern Railway on 1st December 1858. The other lines in the Reading area received third rails on 1st October 1861 and the broad gauge was finally abolished on 21st May 1892.

Quadrupling of the main line was completed thus: Didcot to Cholsey on 27th December 1892, Cholsey to Goring on 27th March 1893, Goring to Pangbourne on 9th July 1893, Pangbourne to Reading West Junction on 30th July 1893 and through Reading in 1899.

The Wallingford branch was authorised under an Act of 25th July 1864, but the ultimate goal of Watlington was never reached. The line opened on 2nd July 1866 and was laid to standard gauge. The Wallingford & Watlington Railway was worked by the GWR and purchased by it in December 1872. Passenger services were withdrawn on 15th June 1959, but freight continued until 13th September 1965.

There were no major changes when the GWR was nationalised in 1948, to become the Western Region of British Railways. Trains began to appear in sector liveries - InterCity and Network SouthEast - in the mid-1980s - these being followed in the mid-1990s by Thames Trains and Great Western Trains colours as a prelude to privatisation. The former franchise was let on 13th October 1996 and the latter on 4th February of the same year; the owning companies became Victory Railway Holdings and First Group respectively. Virgin Cross Country trains run over the route, but only a small proportion call at Didcot.

Most of the Wallingford branch was retained to serve a private siding until 31st May 1981. The Cholsey & Wallingford Railway Preservation Society was formed that year. It steadily increased its running distance and operated into Cholsey from 1999. (See pictures 68-69 and 86-87).

PASSENGER SERVICES

Down trains operating on at least five days per week are shown in the tables below. Fast refers to trains calling at both Reading and Didcot but running non-stop between them. Slow indicates trains calling at least at one intermediate station. Since the 1870s, most slow trains have stopped at all stations.

	Weekdays		Sundays	
	Fast	Slow	Fast	Slow
1848	2	9	-	-
1869	4	5	-	3
1889	7	8	2	4
1909	7	11	5	6
1929	16	16	7	7

Almost all trains ran the full length of the route. However, the final figure in the last column was supplemented by a railmotor making three trips between Reading and Goring & Streatley only.

The train frequency was subject to almost continuous improvement and in the 1960s a regular interval timetable was developed, although with two hour gaps for stopping trains at some periods. From May 1969, this service was hourly. A half-hourly local timetable was introduced in May 1990.

Wallingford branch

Initially there were nine weekday trains, with three on Sundays. The 1869 timetable showed seven trains on weekdays, two of which originated at Reading, and there were three on Sundays. By 1880 there were eight, including two from Reading, but none on Sundays. There were no Sunday trains shown in the following samples of frequencies and very few from Reading.

1895	8
1910	13
1924	15
1938	18
1947	14
1958	11

The branch train was for long known as simply "The Bunk".

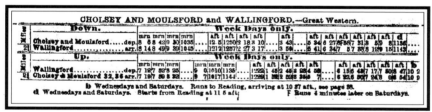

July 1924

July 1958

READING

Goods Station

Station

Rifle Factory

Station

Terminus

Livery Stables

Hotel

18

Royal Horse and Carriage Repository

GARRARD STREET

Malthouse

BLAGRAVE STREET

Workhouse

Battle Farm

A B

BROAD

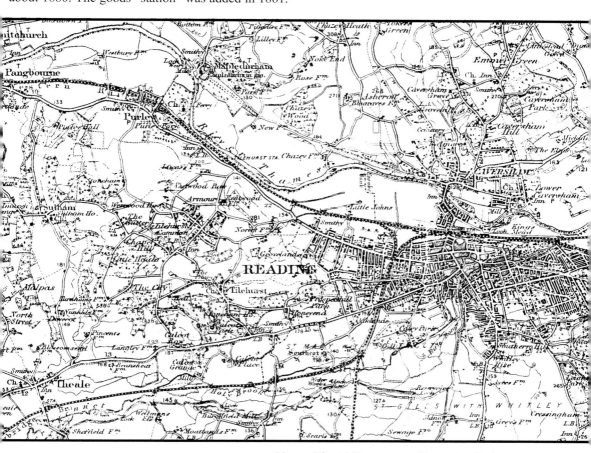

III. The 1st edition reveals that the GWR had two stations - one for up trains and one for down, but both were on the down side. The terminus (right) was for the SER. The two GWR platforms were joined together and the wagon turntables, together with their short sidings, were eliminated in 1861. Complete rebuilding took place in 1865-68, but the engine shed (top left) was in use until about 1880. The goods "station" was added in 1861.

IV. The 1883 survey at 6ins to 1 mile has the route to Didcot top left.

V. The 1901 survey at 1ins to 1 mile has our route to Didcot top left, the London lines on the right, the Basingstoke branch bottom centre and the Westbury route lower left. The Coley branch to the Central Goods Depot did not open until 1908.

1.	This eastward view from 1919 shows the arrangement that had existed since 1899, when the number of platforms was increased from four to ten. The roof of Middle Box is included. There were 398 employed by the GWR at Reading in 1913. (LGRP/NRM)

2.	The improvements included provision of three through lines between the platform roads. Using one of them is 4-4-0 no. 3451 *Pelican*, one of the "Bulldog" class introduced in 1898. (J.G.Sturt)

3.	The London end of the station is seen from Main Line East Box and on the right is the connection to the vast Vastern Road Yard, which had 28 sidings. These were lifted in stages in 1960-72. The box had 115 levers and was in use until 26th April 1965. (M.W.Earley/NRM)

4.   A lengthy up freight on 17th September 1951 passes the 21-lever Middle Box, which closed on 6th June 1959. No. 3841 is at platform 6, which was renumbered 9 in 1955. Until that time, three pairs of platforms had the same number. (D.B.Clayton)

5.   No. 7011 departs from platform 4 with the 11.15 Paddington to Worcester in August 1963. Its exhaust is about to obscure Main Line West Box. The station was named "Reading General" from 26th September 1949 until 6th May 1973. (R.C.Riley/Transport Treasury)

6.   The complex signalling at the west end of the station is evident on 2nd March 1963, as an up express passes over Caversham Road, hauled by no. 7026 *Tenby Castle*. Lower right is the line to platform 7; the connection from it and the short siding were taken out in 1965. (A.E.Bennett)

7. The down and up goods lines and pilot line can be seen in front of the panel box in this 1967 view from Western Tower. Immediately behind the panel box is the station approach road up side. The portion of the double storey building on the far left of the photograph is part of the railway hostel and canteen. Attached to the right of the canteen is part of Reading Works, which later became the outdoor machinery depot. Behind the canteen, part of the Reading S&T department main block can be seen. The top floor was the clock and telegraph shops. The second floor was part of the S&T stores. The Reading signal works, which in its heyday employed over 500 men, stretches across the centre of the photograph. The chimney in the centre forms part of the boiler house which supplied hot water for all of the S&T complex. The containers and freight wagons are in Vastern Road coal yard. Everything beyond the up approach road has long since disappeared. The signal department office block and signal works is now occupied by the Royal Mail main sorting office. The coal yard has been redeveloped as a retail and leisure park. (L.Crosier)

8. A trailing view shows the "South Wales Pullman" (09.00 Paddington-Swansea) as it arrives at platform 4 on 26th March 1973. Introduced in 1959, these 8-car diesel units ceased operation on the Western Region on 5th May 1973. (S.P.Derek)

9. Converted from a former Derby "Lightweight" DMU, the ultrasonic test train (vehicle numbers DB975007 and DB975008) approaches from the west while working from Swindon to Paddington on 11th February 1981. On the right, no. 47528 waits to take over an inter-regional working from Poole to Liverpool. (G.Gillham)

10.   Main Line West Box (210 levers) had ceased to function when colour light signals were introduced on 26th April 1965. However, it was still standing (left) when an HST was recorded arriving from the west on 27th September 1981. Most trains stopped at Reading by that time. (T.Heavyside)

11.   No. 50024 *Vanguard* stands at platform 5 with a train from Oxford on 16th February 1985. On the left, a train for Waterloo waits to depart from platform 4a, which came into use on 6th September 1965, when the former SER terminus was closed. Extreme left is 4b, which opened on 4th May 1975, as having only one platform had given rise to congestion and delays. (A.Dasi-Sutton)

12.   One of the major features today is the huge footbridge that connects the multi storey car park on the northern side of the tracks to the ticket office and circulating area, the Brunel Centre, to the south. It also gives access to the platforms. No. 47645 *Robert F. Fairlie, Locomotive Engineer 1831-1885* departs with the 10.23 Oxford to Paddington service on October 24th 1987. At this time the new station was under construction. (M.Turvey)

13.   The footbridge passes over the goods lines which were retained on the north side of the station. Photographed from platform 10 (a bay used by local trains) on 6th October 1993 was no. 37101. The 1965 signalling centre is in the background. (M.Turvey)

14.   Reading is noted for its diverse destinations. Seen on 14th July 1996 is no. 47806 at platform 9 with the 15.05 Poole to Manchester Piccadilly, while at no. 8 is the 15.10 Great Malvern to Paddington. The centre road was used for running round locomotives of north-south services. (P.G.Barnes)

15.   The spacious new entrance building was opened by Queen Elizabeth II on 4th April 1989, it greatly reducing the congestion caused by the increasing number of airline passengers using the station. The name MENZIES was familiar to rail travellers for generations, but W.H.Smith took over and abandoned the traditional sale of railway books. The picture is from April 1998. (M.J.Stretton)

16.　　Two views from 8th November 1998 feature major track alterations at the junction with the Westbury lines. A class 47 is arriving with the 08.45 Wolverhampton to Poole service. Such trains were often diverted from the Basingstoke route to the Portsmouth line. (M.J.Stretton)

17.　　Not seen in other views herein are platforms 1-3 (right) and 7 (left). No. 66017 is heading the ballast train, while on the points to platform 5 is a tamper with its aligning outrigger retracted. Track alterations were made in 2000 to enable the new shorter north-south trains to reverse at platform 3 instead of 8 and to use the main lines to and from Didcot. (M.J.Stretton)

18.　　No. 47830 departs on 31st July 2000 with Great Western's 12.03 (Summer only) Paddington to Penzance passenger and Motorail service. The specially adapted vans enable the side-loading of cars and for them to be conveyed under cover, in contrast to the facility offered in the 1970s. (S.P.Derek)

READING SHED

19.	A second engine shed had been built within the triangular junction by 1880. Its central turntable is seen here on 23rd August 1930, just prior to the demolition of the building. (H.C.Casserley)

20.	The third shed had three roof-spans covering nine parallel tracks and was recorded on 26th April 1959 in the company of ex-Midland & South Western Junction Railway 2-4-0 no. 1335. There was a 65ft turntable outside its west end. (Wessex coll.)

21.   The coal stage was on the south side of the engine shed and some of the wagons are marked LOCO, being retained exclusively for this traffic. A three-road diesel depot was built in the background in 1959 and enlarged in 1964. (Wessex coll.)

22.   No. 5002 *Ludlow Castle* stands at the east end of the shed on 12th May 1964, with a well loaded tender. Steam traction ended here on 2nd January 1965 and the shed was demolished to make way for permanent way sidings. (H.C.Casserley)

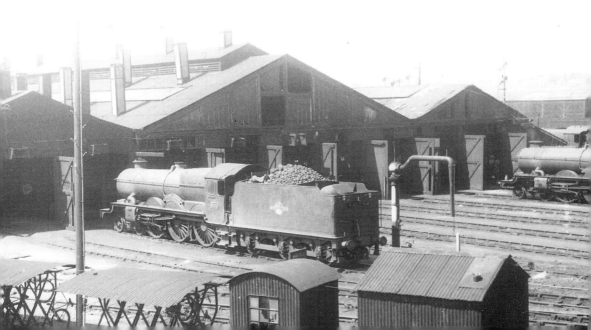

23.   An open day was held at the diesel depot on 19th June 1971 and no. 7808 *Cookham Manor* was attached to two autocoaches. One could ride therein for 5p or on the footplate for 20p. The sleeping car was one of those operating to Paris and Brussels from Victoria on the "Night Ferry". It had coal fired central heating and a lifebelt above each bunk. (S.P.Derek)

24.   Another well attended open day was on 1st June 1985, when the wheel-less no. 31158 was shown on the jacks. It is in the then new Railfreight livery. (M.J.Stretton)

25.   Seen from a train bound for Westbury on 4th August 2001 is the diesel depot, which had been enlarged further in 1981. The steam shed had been right of centre; our route to Didcot is on the extreme right. There was no excess vegetation in steam days. (V.Mitchell)

WEST OF READING

26.   We now look north from almost the same viewpoint as the last picture, but on 12th May 1964. No. 9450 is in front of Reading Goods Lines West Box, which closed on 26th April 1965. There were two goods running lines, in addition to the four for passenger trains. (H.C.Casserley)

27.   Moving further west, we can enjoy the signalman's view from Reading West Junction Box which had a massive new 134 lever frame installed in 1915. It was in use until 24th April 1965. The line from Basingstoke is on the right and on the left are the ten sidings of Up New Yard. Beyond it are the seven of Up Old Yard and to the right (beyond the tank) are the 14 of Down Old Yard. About ¾ mile west, and on the south side, was Scours Lane Box, which had 52 levers and closed on the same date. Beyond it were the 12 sidings of Scours Lane Yard, which were lifted in 1968. (M.W.Earley/NRM)

28.   The Experimental Advanced Passenger Train (APT-E) approaches Reading on 3rd August 1975, after a series of high speed tests over a 20-mile section from Swindon. An astonishing 151mph was reached, while a week later a record 152mph was attained. The 4-car set, weighing 150 tons, was powered by ten 300hp gas turbine engines, and provided research and development data for constructing a service prototype train in 1977. In June 1976 it was put on display at the National Railway Museum, York. The photographer included his bicycle to contrast speed of arrival here. (S.P.Derek)

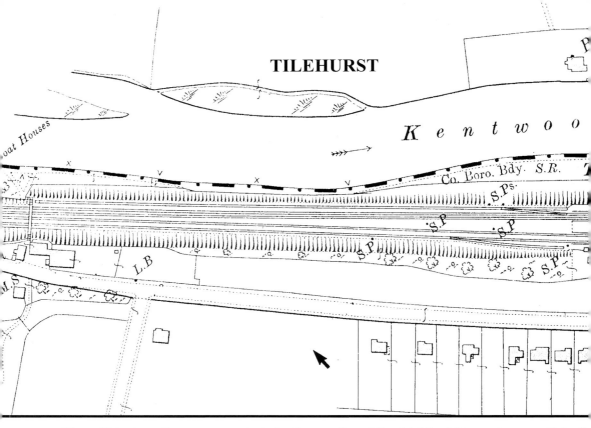

TILEHURST

29.　　This view of an up express includes the up refuge siding (right) which was in use until April 1964. On the left is the engine siding and associated ground frame. These were in situ in 1899-1924. Reference to map V will show that the station, which opened in 1882, was 1½ miles from the village centre. (Lens of Sutton)

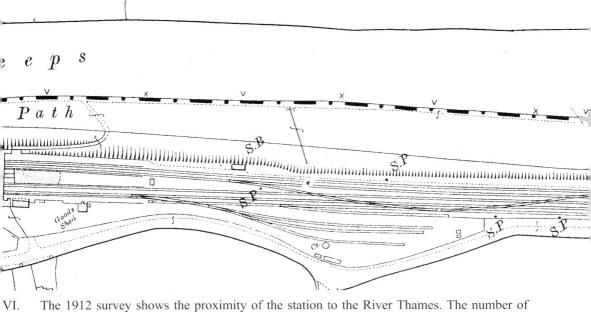

Path

S.B

S.P

S.P

S.P

Goods Shed

Cr. O

S.P

S.P

VI.   The 1912 survey shows the proximity of the station to the River Thames. The number of employees here rose from 8 in 1903 to 13 in 1938. The population was 2418 in 1871, 8863 in 1921 and 19027 in 1991. The GWR extracted a one penny toll from those using the footpath from the up relief platform. The coin had to be inserted in a slot at a turnstile.

30.   The main building and the roof of the station masters house can be seen on the left, while a down stopping train calls on the right. The gardens were well tended, but the lamp was devoid of its gas mantle prior to electrification in the 1960s. The main building and the goods shed are now Listed Grade II. (Lens of Sutton)

31. The platform for up local trains was numbered 4. The signal box had been in the background, but its 53-lever frame was taken out of use on 26th April 1965. It faced the goods yard, which had a 3-ton capacity crane and closed on 7th September 1964. (Lens of Sutton)

32. In the dying months of steam from 1966, steam traction in the Reading area was confined to selected cross-country or through workings between the Southern, and Midland/Eastern Regions One example is the 08.45 Weymouth-Crewe Empty Pigeon Van special in the charge of class 5 4-6-0 no. 45132, on 31st May 1966. (S.P.Derek)

Tilehurst	1903	1913	1923	1933
Passenger tickets issued	12380	17266	21641	21858
Season tickets issued	*	241	433	670
Parcels forwarded	2456	5582	6874	10988
General goods forwarded (tons)	320	1453	909	711
Coal and coke received (tons)	3076	467	1320	575
Other minerals received (tons)	983	693	3180	2656
General goods received (tons)	252	387	1460	1425
Trucks of livestock handled	-	-	-	40
(* not available.)				

33. This January 1968 westward panorama is from the line to the former goods yard. The main building (obscured by the goods shed on the left) is of stone and is older than the others and probably dates from the opening of the station. The building on the right is the oil store. (I.Nash)

34.   An example of Road-Rail integration was the introduction on 18th June 1973 of Reading Corporation's no. 37 "Commuter Bus" service between the station and the village. An AEC awaits the arrival of the 17.42 from Paddington, (due 18.24), while a Brush class 47 speeds by on the down main with the 17.36 Paddington to Swansea on 9th July 1973. The goods shed is behind the bus. (S.P.Derek)

35.   British Rail's prototype class 210 4-car diesel-electric multiple unit intended for suburban duties makes its first revenue trip between Reading and Didcot on Sunday 30th May 1982. Development was overtaken by events, however, and the unit was later converted at the Railway Technical Centre as a Networker prototype train (class 457) to test AC traction motors and their control systems. Three vehicles were later preserved at Coventry, by the Suburban Electric Railway Association. (S.P.Derek)

36.   Oxford services have commonly used the relief lines, this example being the 13.20 from Paddington on 18th April 1992. No. 47581 has just passed the spacious car park that was created on the site of the goods yard. (P.G.Barnes)

37.   The Thames Turbos were introduced in 1992 and represent the third generation of DMUs used in the area. No. 166209 is working the 10.35 Oxford to Paddington stopping service on 8th September 1993. The wooden shelter seen in picture 31 was replaced by a brick structure, following a fire in the late 1970s. (M.J.Stretton)

38.   Mainline Freight liveried no. 37055 *Celebrity* heads the 09.13 Didcot to West Ruislip conveying new Jubilee Line Extension 95 stock, constructed at GEC Alsthom Metro Cammell at Washwood Heath. This regular Thursday working conveyed either new or refurbished London Underground rolling stock and is seen on 11th September 1997. High speed ladder crossings connect all lines to the right of this view. These crossovers are known as "Tilehurst East Junction". (S.P.Derek)

39.   Freight trains tend to be routed on the relief lines, as HSTs speed along the main lines. No. 66124 is hauling empty coal wagons from Didcot Power Station to Southampton Docks on 28th August 2001. Imported coal was a new traffic that year. (J.S.Petley)

40.　　BR class 4 2-6-4Ts nos 80079 and 80098 speed beneath the footbridge with "The Inter City Tanks" charter from Finsbury Park to Gloucester on 22nd May 1999. Unlike so many footbridges, its roof was still complete. The building on the right pre-dates the quadrupling. (S.P.Derek)

WEST OF TILEHURST

41.　　After being on display at the Reading Maintenance Depot Open Day, preserved GWR 2-6-2T no. 5572 heads a special freight back to the Didcot Railway Centre, conveying the Science Museum's replica broad gauge locomotive *Iron Duke* (with chimney removed) and its tender, on two well-wagons, also, the GW Society's preserved ex-GWR railcar no. 22. The assembly is in Purley Cutting on 2nd June 1985. (S.P.Derek)

PANGBOURNE

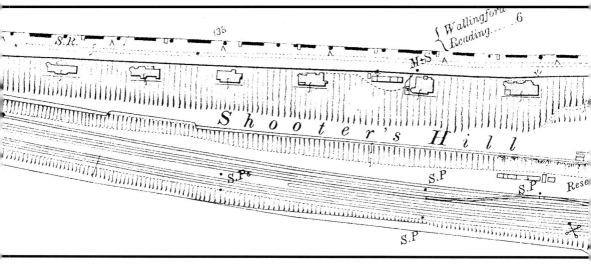

VII.   The 1910 survey shows the main road passing under the tracks near the east end of the island platform. The nearby gasworks was built in 1862 on land purchased from the GWR; it was in use until 1924. The dots and dashes indicate that only the Swan Inn was in the adjacent county of Oxfordshire.

42.   A drawing by J.C.Bourne shows the typical chalet-style that could be enjoyed at most intermediate stations on the route until the quadrupling of 1893. The toll bridge over the Thames can be seen on the left. (M.Dart coll.)

(lower right) 43.The generous ventilation provision for gentlemen is evident in this view of the up relief platform. The local population rose from 1235 in 1901 to 1953 in 1961, while staffing levels increased from 9 in 1903 to 11 in 1933. (Lens of Sutton coll.)

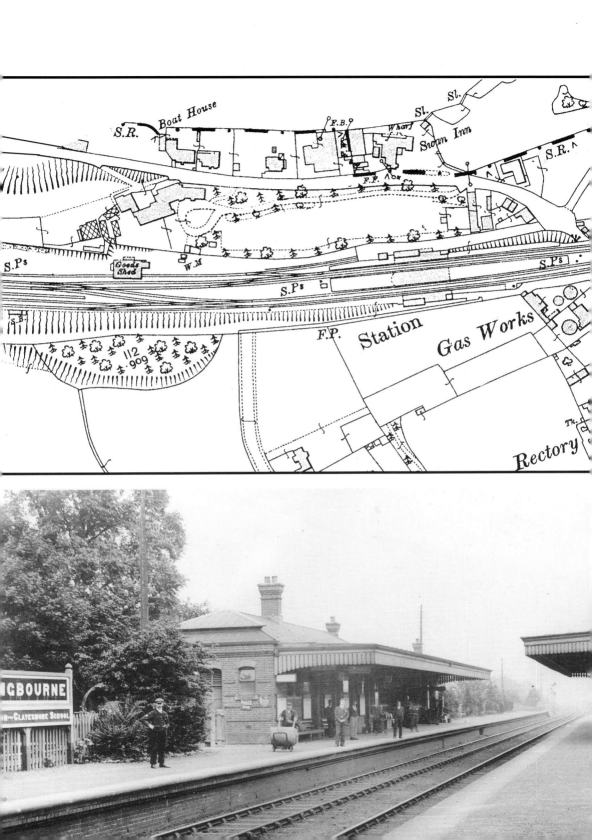

44.　A novel form of track signalling was introduced on 11th August 1907 which avoided the use of an extra signal box to increase line capacity. Semi-automatic electrically operated signals were worked by track circuits, then a new concept, and were situated at Basildon, west of the station. Another set, east thereof at Purley, was provided on 7th August 1910. The batteries were exchanged by a special train every Monday morning until 1952. They were re-charged at Reading Signal Works. The 59-lever signal box is in the distance in this 1919 view. (LGRP/NRM)

45.　The box was in use from 1893 until 9th May 1965. Passing it on 28th March 1962 is no. 6018 *King Henry VI*, with the up "Red Dragon". A wagon stands on the centre siding on the right. (I.Nash)

Pangbourne	1903	1913	1923	1933
Passenger tickets issued	62244	60858	71166	71535
Season tickets issued	*	378	570	725
Parcels forwarded	18098	23138	15782	13953
General goods forwarded (tons)	1622	2071	1132	6285
Coal and coke received (tons)	1540	986	505	870
Other minerals received (tons)	2230	5426	1446	2355
General goods received (tons)	3151	3356	3484	1240
Trucks of livestock handled	113	135	139	8

(* not available.)

46.　Nos. 47258 and 47206 pass the site of the goods yard on 2nd June 1990, hauling a Freightliner from Southampton to Lawley Street, Birmingham. The yard had a 30cwt crane and closed on 7th September 1964. (P.G.Barnes)

47.   A September 1996 photograph includes no. 166203 departing for Paddington and the fence erected on the island platform, as the other face of it had been removed. Both main lines had been realigned northwards slightly in 1975, to reduce the track curvature for HSTs. (F.Hornby)

48.   The exterior was similar to some of the other intermediate stations on the route. Its Victorian ambience had been enhanced when photographed in 1996 by the provision of Sugg's Windsor-style lamps, albeit electrically illuminated. (F.Hornby)

SOUTH OF GORING

49.   To celebrate the launch of "Harry Potter and the Goblet of Fire", a promotion special titled "The Hogwarts Express" was run, using "West Country" class 4-6-2 no. 34027 *Taw Valley*, renamed *Hogwarts Express*, and specially repainted for the event in a shade of maroon not unlike that of the LMS. Speeding along the Thames Valley on 8th July 2000 on the first leg of its 4-day, 1200 mile journey from London Kings Cross to Perth, it ran via Didcot, the Severn Valley Railway, Manchester, York, Newcastle and Edinburgh, with "The Pride of the Nation" charter train coaches. (S.P.Derek)

<table>
<tr><td>

956

Gt Western Ry   Gt Western Ry
Pangbourne   Pangbourne
GORING TO & Streatley
FIRST CLASS
9d Fare 9d
Issue i subject to the conditions & regulations set
out in the Company's Time Tables Bills & Notices
Goring & Streatley   Goring & Streatley

956

</td><td>

3745

Gt Western Ry   Gt Western Ry
Pangbourne   Pangbourne
STEVENTON TO
THIRD CLASS
1/11   Fare   1/11
Issued subject to the conditions & regulations set
out in the Company's Time Tables Bills & Notices
Steventon   Steventon

3745

</td></tr>
</table>

50.   Water troughs for the collection of water at speed were established on the level track east of the 143yd long Gatehampton Viaduct over the Thames. Class 3232 2-4-0 no. 3235 is passing over them with a train of horseboxes on 13th March 1915. (K.Nunn/LCGB)

51.   No. 5042 Winchester Castle is picking up water on 15th September 1958. Nearby were two sidings serving the water softening plant. The 620yd-long troughs were brought into use (on the relief lines) on 30th June 1898. They all ceased to be used in 1965. (R.S.Carpenter)

Brewery

W
60
W
W

GORING & STREATLEY

S.P
S.P

Flint
W
S.P

Sloane Hotel

Queen's Arms
(P.H)
P

Goring Farm

School
W

L.B

Goring & Streatley Station

P
P
erance
ll

P

S.P
S.P

171

P
P

C
R
O
F
T

S.P
S.P

S.P
Cattle Pens

L.B

171

III.   The 1897 survey has the main road
nder the platforms. It continues west
cross a toll bridge over the river.

Goring & Streatley	1903	1913	1923	1933
assenger tickets issued	57649	49818	56991	51433
eason tickets issued	*	*	488	804
arcels forwarded	20075	23857	17171	17035
eneral goods forwarded (tons)	1870	3929	2649	969
oal and coke received (tons)	450	346	758	899
ther minerals received (tons)	1199	1703	2473	986
eneral goods received (tons)	3589	3857	2346	1003
rucks of livestock handled	142	135	69	35

* not available.)

Cr

S.P

S.P

S.Ps

52.   Below the left part of the footbridge can be seen the connection to the goods yard, which had a 6-ton crane and was open until 7th September 1965. Trailing from the down main line (right) are points for a refuge siding, which was in use until 1964. The photograph is from 1919; around this time about 10 or 11 men were employed here. (LGRP/NRM)

53.   The suffix was added on 9th November 1895; by 1901 Goring housed 1419 souls and Streatley 562. Generous provision for the weather protection of passengers was made. However, the nearest canopy was primarily to keep the rain off parcels. (Lens of Sutton coll.)

54.   Colour light signals came into use when the 65-lever signal box closed on 9th May 1965. Running on the up relief line on 22nd October 1988 is no. L243 working the 14.24 Oxford to Reading. The road passes over the tracks and leads to a bridge across the Thames (P.G.Barnes)

55.   A Speedlink service was recorded on 11th July 1990 as no. 47100 was working assorted wagons from Southampton to Haverton Hill, Middlesbrough. The cutting was necessary owing to a meander in the Thames bringing it close to the eroded Chalk of the Chilterns. (S.P.Derek)

56.   Economies are evident as no. 165101 departs for Reading on 26th September 1996 - mirrors to allow one-person-operation of trains and cut-back of passenger weather protection provisions. West of the station, there had been an intermediate six-lever signal box at South Stoke from about 1917 to 1920. Another was provided from 1940-1953; it had a 14-lever frame. (F.Hornby)

MOULSFORD

57.   The station was known as Wallingford Road until the Wallingford branch opened on 2nd July 1866, when a bay platform and footbridge were added. Moulsford had a timetable curiosity in its final years: a train ran from Reading on the 3rd Friday of each month, terminating there at 10.48am. This junction closed on 29th February 1892 during the provision of quadruple track. There had been an independent track for ¾ mile westwards before the branch turned northwards. (M.Pooley coll.)

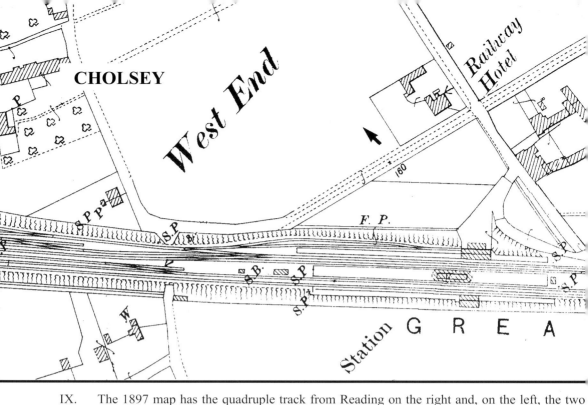

CHOLSEY

IX.   The 1897 map has the quadruple track from Reading on the right and, on the left, the two pairs are separated by a refuge siding. Above them are two further sidings and the curve of the Wallingford branch.

58.   An early postcard view includes the barrow crossing, but a subway was provided for passengers. The station opened on 29th February 1892, following the closure of Moulsford. (Lens of Sutton)

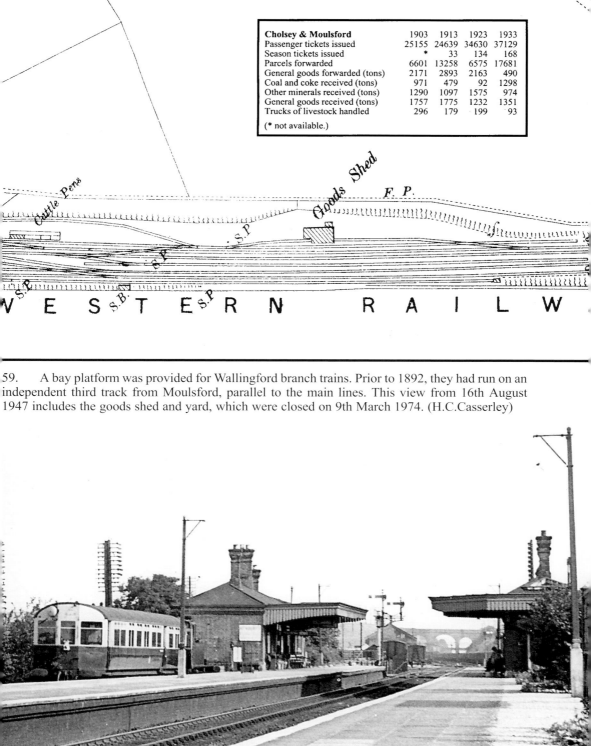

Cholsey & Moulsford	1903	1913	1923	1933
Passenger tickets issued	25155	24639	34630	37129
Season tickets issued	*	33	134	168
Parcels forwarded	6601	13258	6575	17681
General goods forwarded (tons)	2171	2893	2163	490
Coal and coke received (tons)	971	479	92	1298
Other minerals received (tons)	1290	1097	1575	974
General goods received (tons)	1757	1775	1232	1351
Trucks of livestock handled	296	179	199	93

(* not available.)

59.   A bay platform was provided for Wallingford branch trains. Prior to 1892, they had run on an independent third track from Moulsford, parallel to the main lines. This view from 16th August 1947 includes the goods shed and yard, which were closed on 9th March 1974. (H.C.Casserley)

60.   The train in the previous picture is shown in close-up. It is the 4.35pm from Wallingford and is formed of 0-4-2T no. 1447 and autocoach no. 194. This service was withdrawn on 15th June 1959. (H.C.Casserley)

61.   The 12.50pm up train was recorded arriving from Didcot on 18th June 1949. The lighting was in transition with the new electric lights and the old posts for pressurised oil lamps standing simultaneously. (J.H.Meredith)

62.   Passengers from the arriving branch train who were bound for Didcot would access the subway via the arch to the right of the seat. The signal box (left) replaced two on 23rd July 1908. West Box had been in the distance. Both are shown on the map. (Lens of Sutton coll.)

63. The run-round loop was in place until 1963 although little used. With autotrains in use for many years, it had not been used much previously either. Ten men had been employed here between the wars. (Lens of Sutton)

64. The signal box had 75 levers and functioned until 9th May 1965. Its size necessitated two stoves; however, such boxes were still cold in winter owing to sliding windows and draughts through the frame slots. (Lens of Sutton)

65. On Saturday 21st September 1968, the Great Western Society held an Open Day on the Wallingford Branch, with a static display of rolling stock and trips to and from Wallingford with their 0-4-2T no. 1466 and autocoach no. 231. The connection between the up relief line and branch was removed in 1981, the same year that the Cholsey & Wallingford Railway Preservation Society was founded. (S.P.Derek)

66.   In conjunction with Wallingford Carnival, on Saturday 21st June 1969, the Great Western Society ran a special DMU service, seen here waiting in the bay platform. (S.P.Derek)

67.   The 12.18 Manchester Piccadilly to Paddington speeds through behind a class 47 on 29th February 1992, the 100th anniversary of the station. This explains the bunting and the period policeman. The main entrance is at subway level. (M.Turvey)

68.   After years of hard work nearer Wallingford, the CWRPS ran into the bay on 27th July 1996 behind a class J94 (numbered fictitiously 68006) with a class 08 diesel on the other end. They had also done so on 15th December 1994, but it was to be 1999 before regular operation commenced. (M.Turvey)

69.   A Polish 0-6-0T appeared in the bay on 16th August 1998 with the society's three MkI coaches. Note that the loop had been restored, although there was not one at the other end of the line. (D.Trevor Rowe)

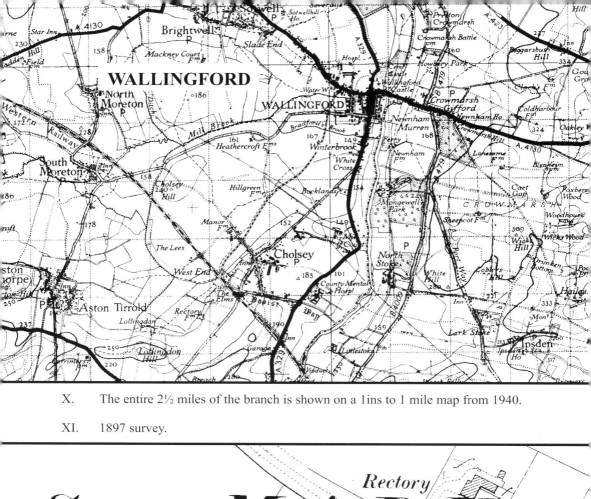

X.   The entire 2½ miles of the branch is shown on a 1ins to 1 mile map from 1940.

XI.   1897 survey.

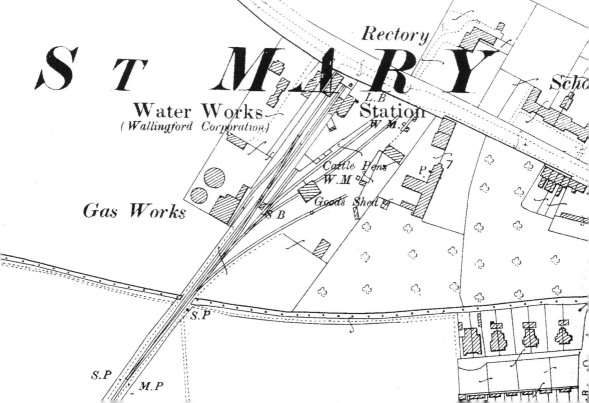

70.   The prospective passengers perspective was recorded on a postcard and includes the 1885 waterworks tower and part of the 1876 gasworks. The population had only reached 2808 by 1901 and was about 5000 when passenger services ceased. There was a staff of 10 or 12 between 1903 and 1938. (Lens of Sutton)

71.   The entrance was on the right of the previous picture and another postcard features its massive gateposts, together with the gate. Horse droppings were a smelly nuisance at the approach to most stations. (Lens of Sutton)

Wallingford	1903	1913	1923	1933
Passenger tickets issued	43093	40729	44762	29079
Season tickets issued	*	35	153	132
Parcels forwarded	34566	38100	33083	41334
General goods forwarded (tons)	7833	6892	7607	1540
Coal and coke received (tons)	963	852	652	1815
Other minerals received (tons)	2611	4945	4265	5336
General goods received (tons)	7439	7943	7933	4996
Trucks of livestock handled	221	533	261	105
(* not available.)				

72.   This 1919 panorama includes the engine shed which replaced the original one in 1890. A spare coach stands in the dock, which has an end loading facility. There was a well to supply locomotive water and the pump was housed in the shed beyond the nearest gas lamp. The canopy dates from 1891. The branch engine provided steam for it via a hose. (LGRP/NRM)

73.   The end-loading dock and pump house are shown more clearly in this photograph from June 1949. A mixed train has just arrived and the crew watch the coach being uncoupled. The 3000 gallon water tank had replaced the one seen in the previous picture in 1920. (J.H.Meredith)

74.   An autocoach approaches the end of its journey and passes a wagon standing on the line leading to the gasworks. Its private siding was closed on 29th June 1953; the gas lamp had been fitted with a shade as a wartime blackout measure. (Lens of Sutton)

75.   The spacious lean-to provided for the convenience of gentlemen is the main feature of this November 1956 view. Also seen are a Ford Prefect and an Austin lorry. (R.M.Casserley)

WALLINGFORD STATION BOX

77.   The signal box remained in use until 19th January 1964, almost five years after the last passenger train had left. It was worked by the senior porter. (B.W.Leslie/GWS)

76.   Passengers chat while the fireman hangs on the water valve chain on 14th August 1957. The water feed pipe is insulated, but a "Fire Devil" is provided to prevent the tank freezing. An electric pump had been installed by that time. (H.C.Casserley)

78.　　　The locomotive shed was closed on 11th February 1956 and an engine came each weekday from Didcot subsequently. Reading engines were used prior to about 1933. The gas lamp had been replaced by one of Sugg's Rochester pattern. At the end of the platform is the oil store, bicycle shed and parcels office. (R.S.Carpenter)

79.	Tender engines, such as this class 2251 0-6-0, were rarely used on the branch. This example was photographed on 7th June 1958, at a time when steam was being reduced and engine availability was poor. (E.Wilmshurst)

80.	Three photos from 9th September 1966 show the trackwork in detail and that points were then worked by hand. A stream passes under the tracks our side of the loading gauge. The engine shed was demolished in 1971. (R.S.Carpenter)

81.	Goods handling had ceased on 13th September 1965. Outward traffic had been locally built trailers and agricultural equipment, plus scrap metal. Inwards was the usual coal, fertiliser and building materials. (R.S.Carpenter)

82.   The loop had been extended twice, in 1927 and 1941. A siding was added in the distance, on the right, for milk traffic and was in use from 1933 until 1962. The station and yard area was developed for housing and the branch was cut back to the tall building of Associated British Maltsters (Southern) Ltd. (left). This was provided with sidings on 13th July 1961, soon after the mill was completed. (R.S.Carpenter)

83.   The Great Western Society's 0-4-2T was in steam at the mill on 15th April 1968. Its autocoach is on the points to the two sidings. The pair had run in June 1967 for the Wallingford Carnival. (S.C.Nash)

84.   An open day on 15th June 1968 enabled visitors to see no. 6998 *Burton Agnes Hall,* which is normally resident at the Didcot Railway Centre. The sidings were still busy with malt, fertiliser, grain and coal for the plant. (E.Wilmshurst)

85.   A bigger event was staged on 21st September 1968 with no. 1466 again (right), a showmans engine and 2-6-2T no. 6106 (left of centre). The branch was 2¼ miles long by that time; the former running line is on the right. (S.C.Nash)

86.   No platform existed when a special train ran on 31st May 1981 to mark the closure of the branch for freight traffic to the mill. It would be 17th April 1988 before the CWRPS would be able to run its first train. The 0-4-0ST *Uskmouth* was hired to run on a ½ mile length of track. (P.G.Barnes)

87.   Two parallel tracks and a platform existed outside the mill property by the time that this photograph was taken on 29th February 1992. More recently the mill was demolished to make way for housing, but a little more land was acquired for the terminus. A Light Railway Order was obtained in 1990 and 1¼ miles of track were in use by 1993. A bypass for the town was built across the line in 1995 and a level crossing with automatic barriers was provided. (M.Turvey)

88.   Moreton Cutting signal box is above the rear coach of the up "Bristolian" on 22nd September, 1961. Beyond it are the 16 sidings of the yard which was in use from 1941 until 1964. "Warship" class diesel hydraulic no. D839 *Relentless* speeds east, while WD "Austerity" 2-8-0 no. 90565 waits to leave the yard. The goods line on the right joins the up relief line, almost two miles from Didcot station. The 90-lever box closed on 17th May 1965. Aston Tirrold box was almost a mile further east; it had 14 levers and was in use from 1940 to 1954. (M.Mensing/M.J.Stretton coll.)

Didcot	1903	1913	1923	1933
Passenger tickets issued	37860	45471	73701	96476
Season tickets issued	*	140	352	750
Parcels forwarded	14775	16883	23568	45597
General goods forwarded (tons)	6158	6091	23592	17131
Coal and coke received (tons)	96	33	584	3268
Other minerals received (tons)	1942	1093	7282	8750
General goods received (tons)	6075	7757	17241	15359
Trucks of livestock handled	283	629	544	88

(* not available.)

DIDCOT PARKWAY

89.   The station opened as simply "Didcot" on 12th June 1844, four years after the main line was completed. Its purpose was to serve as the junction for Oxford. It had four through passenger lines and six platform faces. The elegant wooden building lasted about 40 years. (LGRP/NRM)

90.   The south elevation was the subject of a postcard produced around 1900 and it includes one of the two bay platforms on this side of the station; the other is in the next picture. They remained in use until 1968. The staff level rose from 120 in 1903 to 153 in 1938. (Lens of Sutton)

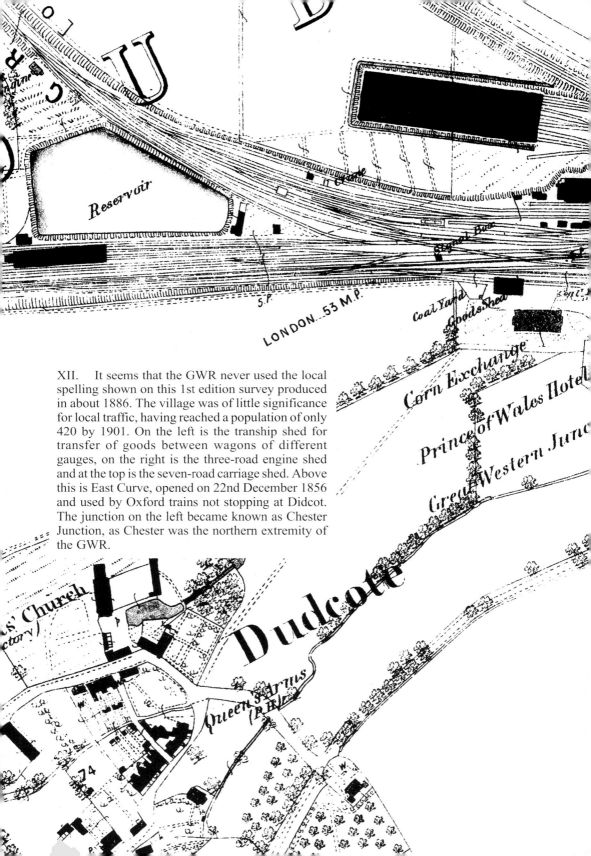

XII.   It seems that the GWR never used the local spelling shown on this 1st edition survey produced in about 1886. The village was of little significance for local traffic, having reached a population of only 420 by 1901. On the left is the tranship shed for transfer of goods between wagons of different gauges, on the right is the three-road engine shed and at the top is the seven-road carriage shed. Above this is East Curve, opened on 22nd December 1856 and used by Oxford trains not stopping at Didcot. The junction on the left became known as Chester Junction, as Chester was the northern extremity of the GWR.

Reservoir

LONDON 53 M.P.

S.P.

Coal Yard

Goods Shed

Corn Exchange

Prince of Wales Hotel

Great Western Junc

Dudcote

's Church

Queen's Arms (P.H.)

74

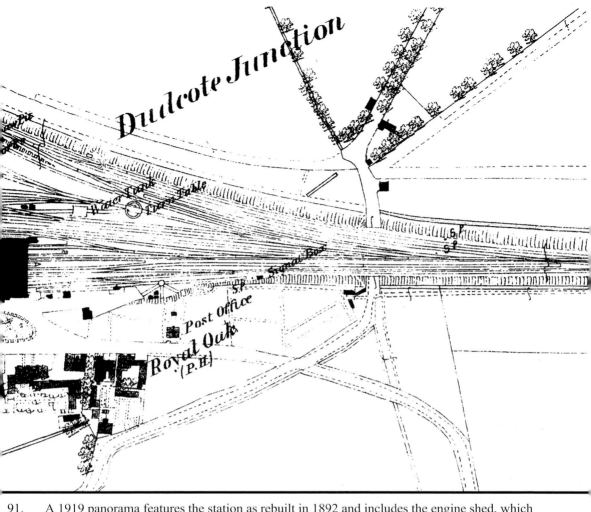

91.   A 1919 panorama features the station as rebuilt in 1892 and includes the engine shed, which lasted until 1932. The line in the foreground was used by Newbury trains and received a run-round loop in 1932. The Corn Exchange (left) is carrying a YMCA sign. (LGRP/NRM)

92.   An eastward view in 1932 includes the bay loop (right), which joins the single line of the former Didcot, Newbury & Southampton Railway which is illustrated in *Didcot to Winchester* (Middleton Press). It was doubled in 1943 and closed in 1964. (LGRP/NRM)

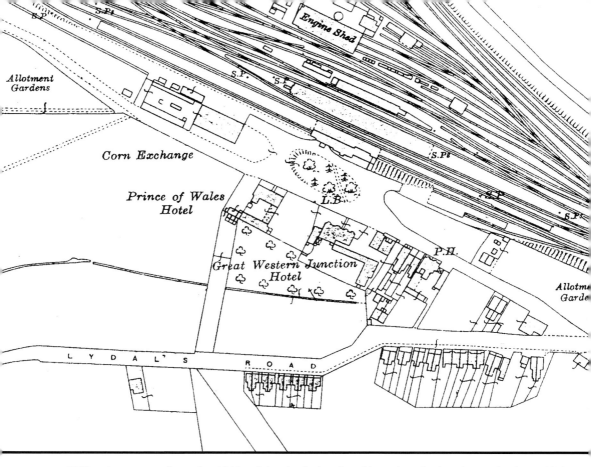

XIII.   An extract from the 1932 edition includes the old engine shed and a track plan which was about to disappear. The Newbury line curves south at the right border and below it are the sidings of Rich's wagon repair works, which were in use from 1928 until 1937. Two signal boxes are shown on the right at East Junction. The old one had 45 levers and the new one had 150. At the end of the long island platform is Didcot East End Box which had 57 levers in use until closure in 1932.

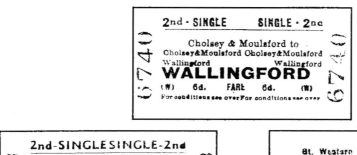

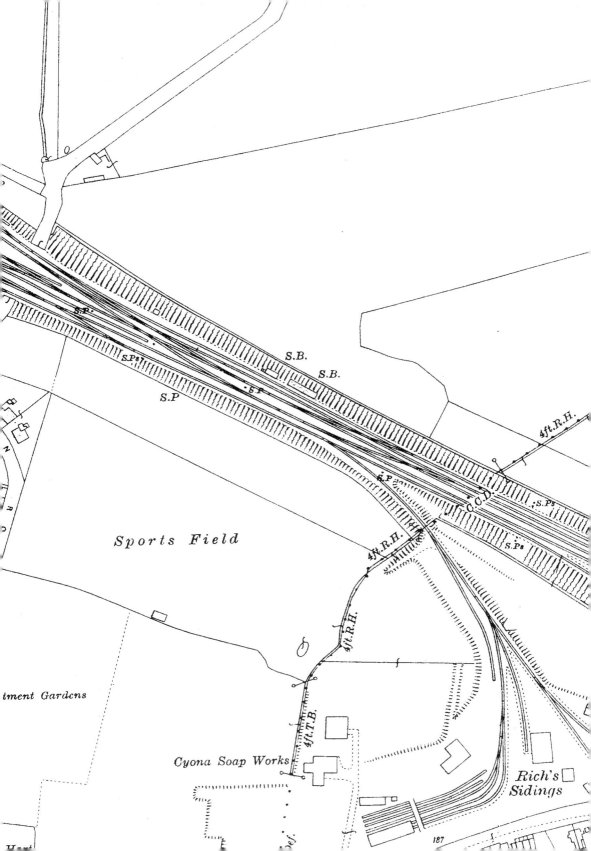

S.P.

S.Ps

S.P

S.B.

S.P.

S.B.

4ft.R.H.

S.P

S.Ps

C.D.

S.Ps

Sports Field

4ft.R.H.

4ft.R.H.

tment Gardens

4ft.T.B.

Cyona Soap Works

Rich's
Sidings

187

93.   Looking west late in 1932, we see the platforms as lengthened and straightened that year. The engine shed was demolished in June of that Summer - its replacement was built further north and is seen on the right. On the skyline is the massive provender mill, which was rail served, and on the right is East Curve. (LGRP/NRM)

94.   The new engine shed is seen in pristine condition on 16th August 1936, with "Bulldog" class no. 3448 *Kingfisher* in attendance. The depot was in use until 16th June 1965. (H.C.Casserley)

95.   An August 1936 photograph features 1901 class no. 2007. "State of the art" would be the modern term to describe the shed. Note the well designed smoke troughs for example. (J.G.Sturt)

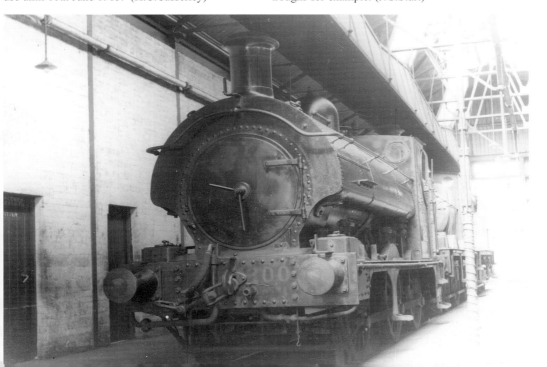

96.   No. 5082 *Swordfish* approaches platform 3 (No. 1 from 1965) with a down express on 16th August 1957. In the distance is East Box, which had a 150-lever frame and was in use until colour light signals arrived on 17th May 1965. See the cover caption for more information. (H.C.Casserley)

97.   Running into platform 1 on 14th September 1974 is no. 47467 with a Paddington to Swansea service. The number of long distance trains calling here has increased greatly over the years. (T.Heavyside)

98.   The suffix "Parkway" was added on 29th July 1985. HSTs were calling regularly, such as no. 253022 which was recorded on 25th September 1982. In the background are parts of Didcot Power Station, which receives vast amounts of coal by rail. A train is on East Curve on the right and to the left of it is the Didcot Railway Centre. (M.Turvey)

99. Modern locomotives are not kept in a shed, merely stood at a "stabling point", devoid of even a stable. Viewed from platform 5 on 7th September 1996 are nos 37798, 37372, 37245, 58011 and 37198. A small depot was established later, further west. (P.G.Barnes)

100. Spacious new buildings were completed in 1985, but the platforms and subway were altered little. Seen in July 2001, the entrance to the Didcot Railway Centre is on the left, visitors using the subway. There is no access for road vehicles to the "rail locked" site. (V.Mitchell)

DIDCOT RAILWAY CENTRE

01.   The Great Western Society was formed in 1961 and collection of historic material began at a number of different locations. The redundant steam depot here was acquired in 1967 and exhibits began to be moved from the other sites. The open day on 20th September 1969 revealed 0-4-0WT no. 5 *Shannon* (left), 2-6-2T no. 6106 and 0-4-2T no. 1466. (S.P.Derek)

GREAT WESTERN RAILWAY

IMPORTANT ❦ ❦ ❦ ❦
❦ ❦ ANNOUNCEMENT

RAILWAY OPEN DAY
AT
DIDCOT M.P.D.
DIDCOT RAILWAY STATION
BERKSHIRE

This joint enterprise of BRITISH RAIL and the GREAT WESTERN SOCIETY will be open between the hours of 11 a.m. and 6.30 p.m. on SATURDAY

SEPTEMBER 18

The Exhibition will include STEAM and DIESEL Locomotives and examples of old and new Rolling Stock. Visitors will be afforded the facility of travel in either of two Steam Trains at a fare of 5p.
PRICE OF ADMISSION 30p Adult, 15p Child

"IT'S QUICKER BY RAIL"

196, Norwood Road,
Southall,
Middx.

KEVIN R. McCORMACK
Secretary
GREAT WESTERN SOCIETY

F.D. 8/71 15,000

Denny Bros., Printers, Bury St. Edmunds

The 1971 publicity handbill from the GWR was in the style of the original company.

102.   On show on 14th September 1974 were GWR railcar no. 4, 0-6-2T no. 6697 and 2-8-2T no. 7202. Most of the stock is owned by the GWS, but some is in private hands and some is part of the national collection, such as the railcar.   (T.Heavyside)

103.   Seen near the north end of the site on 16th August 1980 is the carriage shed and traverser, which came from Derby Works. Although there had been a turntable in this vicinity, the one illustrated was brought from Southampton Docks. (J.H.Meredith)

104.   No. 43106 is a 4MT 2-6-0 built by BR in 1951 and normally resident on the Severn Valley Railway. It had brought an excursion from Birmingham on 27th September 1980 and is being serviced alongside the 1932 coal stage, an important original exhibit on the site. (T.Heavyside)

105.   On show on 26th September 1981 was 0-4-0WT no. 5 from the Wantage Tramway, a relic from 1857 and preserved by the GWR in 1945. On the left is *Lion* which was built in 1838 for the Liverpool & Manchester Railway. It was in the film "The Titfield Thunderbolt" - see our *Frome to Bristol* album. (T.Heavyside)

106.   The GWS had laid some broad gauge and mixed gauge track near the re-erected tranship shed. As part of the Society's 25th anniversary events, it was rightly honoured by a visit of the Science Museum's replica broad gauge 2-2-2 *Iron Duke* on 27th May 1986. Even the signals are correct for the period. (S.P.Derek)

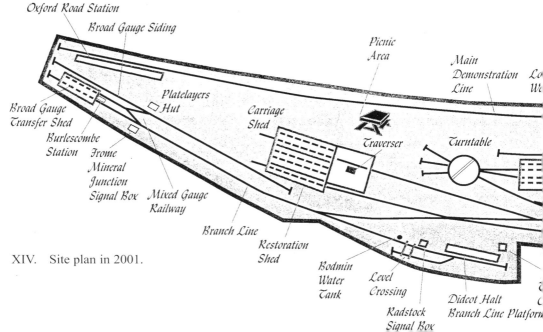

Oxford Road Station

Broad Gauge Siding

Picnic Area

Main Demonstration Line

Lo We

Platelayers Hut

Carriage Shed

Traverser

Turntable

Broad Gauge Transfer Shed

Burlescombe Station

Frome Mineral Junction Signal Box

Mixed Gauge Railway

Branch Line

Restoration Shed

Bodmin Water Tank

Level Crossing

Didcot Halt Branch Line Platform

Radstock Signal Box

XIV.   Site plan in 2001.

107.   The GWS went from strength to strength and was eventually able to operate an authentic GWR freight train. No. 5572 was recorded on 2nd April 1988 with an immaculately restored set of wagons coupled to a traditional GWR "Toad" brake van. (T.Heavyside)

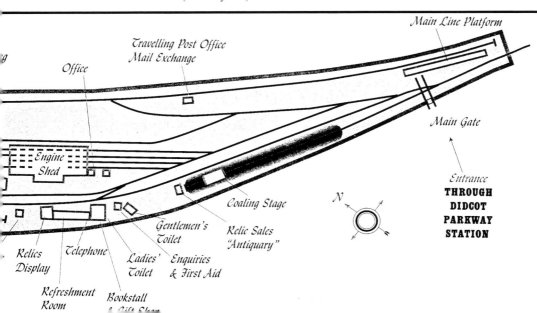

Main Line Platform

Travelling Post Office
Mail Exchange

Office

Engine
Shed

Main Gate

Entrance
**THROUGH
DIDCOT
PARKWAY
STATION**

N

Coaling Stage

Gentlemen's
Toilet

Relic Sales
"Antiquary"

Relics
Display

Telephone

Ladies'
Toilet

Enquiries
& First Aid

Refreshment
Room

Bookstall
& Gift Shop

108.   Later the same day, no. 5572 was working a country branch train into Didcot Halt, which had been created by members and provided with a genuine GWR Pagoda shelter recovered from Stockcross & Bagnor (see *Branch Line to Lambourn*). The signal box had spent its working life at Radstock. (T.Heavyside)

109.   The GWR coded much of its stock after reptiles, fish and amphibians. This is a "Crocodile" and bears the boiler of no. 6023 *King Edward II* on 5th May 1990. In the background is a fully operational GWR steam operated breakdown crane. (M.J.Stretton)

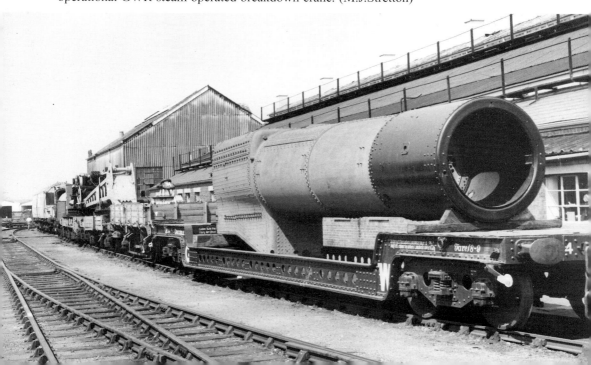

114.   There are projects to develop lost aspects of the GWR. One of these is to recreate a steam railmotor. A[t] the launch of the project on 25th April 1998 Thames Trains loaned turbo diesel multiple unit no. 165125. It was displayed in front of the old steam shed with Great Western diesel railcar no. 22, a push and pull coach and the coach that had been rescued to return to its original design. The GWS has also announced a scheme to build [a] replica "Saint" class 4-6-0 and the replica broad gauge 2-2-2 *Firefly* was under construction by the Firefl[y] Trust. (M.Turvey)

115.   "Castle" class 4-6-0 no. 5051 *Earl Bathurst* is one of the resident locomotives and is seen being turne[d] by hand in the traditional way on 26th September 1998. The locomotive, with tender full, weighs 125 tons. There is a geared mechanism at the other end of the table. (P.G.Barnes)

110.   The original location of the tranship (or transfer) shed is shown on the 1st edtion map. It was moved piece by piece to the north end of the GWS site in 1977, using a Manpower Services Commission grant. Its two doorway sizes reflect its original purpose, although it is now used by passengers starting their journey at the halt shown in picture 108. (M.J.Stretton)

111.   Class 8P 4-6-2 no. 71000 *Duke of Gloucester* was another welcome visitor. It ran from Crewe to Gloucester on 7th November 1992 and is seen on the 11th, the day before working back to the GCR. (M.J.Stretton)

112.   The GWS staged a special RAIL-MAIL event on 23rd September 1995 and were able to demonstrate the old system of mailbag collection at speed. No. 70000 *Britannia* was visiting and is seen performing briskly at the east end of the main running line, near the Eynsham platform. (M.J.Stretton)

113.   As part of the same event, Rail Express Systems showed one of their 16 units devoted to mail traffic. They are capable of running on DC 750 volts or AC 25kV or being diesel hauled. The occasion marked 100 years of the TPO - Travelling Post Office. (M.J.Stretton)

116. Among the interesting variety of special events organised by the GWS are night photography evenings. This impressive result was created on 30th October 1998 and includes WTC no. 5, GWR 0-6-0ST no. 1363 and 2-8-0T no. 4277. (M.J.Stretton)

117. Viewed from platform 5 is the end of the subway (left) from which everyone gains access to the site. The fenced section is across disused sidings in this photograph of no. 4472 *Flying Scotsman* visiting on 2nd June 2000. Plans were being made by the GWS to purchase these tracks and enlarge the site. Behind the sign is Eynsham shelter, which was erected in 1995 on the platform at the southern end of the demonstration main line. (V.Mitchell)

118. A panorama from Eynsham shelter on the same day includes no. 6024 *King Edward I* on the coal road, with 0-6-0PT no. 3738 nearby. In the background is the bookshop, buffet and museum, while on the right stands 0-4-0ST no. 1338 with other exhibits outside the engine shed. The excess vegetation would have been frowned on by the GWR! (V.Mitchell)

119. A comprehensive display of GWR signal and telegraph equipment is seen on the same day, near Frome Mineral Junction signal box. The bridge rail and transoms of broad gauge track are shown well in the foreground. A section of pipe for atmospheric propulsion is on show and appears in picture no. 3 in our *Exeter to Newton Abbot* album. (V.Mitchell)

120. *Trojan* was built for the Alexandra Docks & Railway Company in 1897 and withdrawn by the GWR in 1932. It was photographed in the lifting shop on 5th December 2001 in steam for the first time since a prolonged major overhaul. The GWS never ceases to work wonders and to give pleasure to GWR admirers. (M.J.Stretton)

MP Middleton Press

Easebourne Lane, Midhurst, W Sussex. GU29 9AZ **Tel: 01730 813169 Fax: 01730 812601**
*If books are not available from your local transport stockist, order direct with cheque,
Visa or Mastercard, post free UK.*

BRANCH LINES

Branch Line to Allhallows
Branch Line to Alton
Branch Lines around Ascot
Branch Line to Ashburton
Branch Lines around Bodmin
Branch Line to Bude
Branch Lines around Canterbury
Branch Lines around Chard & Yeovil
Branch Line to Cheddar
Branch Lines around Cromer
Branch Lines to East Grinstead
Branch Lines of East London
Branch Lines to Effingham Junction
Branch Lines around Exmouth
Branch Lines to Falmouth, Helston & St. Ives
Branch Line to Fairford
Branch Lines around Gosport
Branch Line to Hawkhurst
Branch Lines to Horsham
Branch Lines around Huntingdon
Branch Line to Ilfracombe
Branch Line to Kingswear
Branch Line to Lambourn
Branch Lines to Launceston & Princetown
Branch Line to Looe
Branch Line to Lyme Regis
Branch Lines around Midhurst
Branch Line to Minehead
Branch Line to Moretonhampstead
Branch Lines to Newport
Branch Lines to Newquay
Branch Lines around North Woolwich
Branch Line to Padstow
Branch Lines around Plymouth
Branch Lines to Seaton and Sidmouth
Branch Line to Selsey
Branch Lines around Sheerness
Branch Line to Shrewsbury
Branch Line to Swanage *updated*
Branch Line to Tenterden
Branch Lines around Tiverton
Branch Lines to Torrington
Branch Lines to Tunbridge Wells
Branch Line to Upwell
Branch Lines of West London
Branch Lines around Weymouth
Branch Lines around Wimborne
Branch Lines around Wisbech

NARROW GAUGE

Branch Line to Lynton
Branch Lines around Portmadoc 1923-46
Branch Lines around Porthmadog 1954-94
Branch Line to Southwold
Douglas to Port Erin
Kent Narrow Gauge
Northern France Narrow Gauge
Romneyrail
Southern France Narrow Gauge
Sussex Narrow Gauge
Two-Foot Gauge Survivors
Vivarais Narrow Gauge

SOUTH COAST RAILWAYS

Ashford to Dover
Bournemouth to Weymouth
Brighton to Worthing
Eastbourne to Hastings
Hastings to Ashford
Portsmouth to Southampton
Ryde to Ventnor
Southampton to Bournemouth

SOUTHERN MAIN LINES

Basingstoke to Salisbury
Bromley South to Rochester
Crawley to Littlehampton
Dartford to Sittingbourne
East Croydon to Three Bridges
Epsom to Horsham
Exeter to Barnstaple
Exeter to Tavistock
Faversham to Dover
London Bridge to East Croydon
Orpington to Tonbridge
Salisbury to Yeovil
Swanley to Ashford
Tavistock to Plymouth
Three Bridges to Brighton
Victoria to Bromley South
Victoria to East Croydon
Waterloo to Windsor
Waterloo to Woking
Woking to Portsmouth
Woking to Southampton
Yeovil to Exeter

EASTERN MAIN LINES

Ely to Kings Lynn
Fenchurch Street to Barking
Ipswich to Saxmundham
Liverpool Street to Ilford
Saxmundham to Yarmouth

WESTERN MAIN LINES

Ealing to Slough
Exeter to Newton Abbot
Newton Abbot to Plymouth
Newbury to Westbury
Paddington to Ealing
Plymouth to St. Austell
Slough to Newbury
St. Austell to Penzance

COUNTRY RAILWAY ROUTES

Andover to Southampton
Bath Green Park to Bristol
Bath to Evercreech Junction
Bournemouth to Evercreech Jn.
Cheltenham to Andover
Croydon to East Grinstead
Didcot to Winchester
East Kent Light Railway
Fareham to Salisbury

Guildford to Redhill
Reading to Basingstoke
Reading to Guildford
Redhill to Ashford
Salisbury to Westbury
Stratford upon Avon to Cheltenham
Strood to Paddock Wood
Taunton to Barnstaple
Wenford Bridge to Fowey
Westbury to Bath
Woking to Alton
Yeovil to Dorchester

GREAT RAILWAY ERAS

Ashford from Steam to Eurostar
Clapham Junction 50 years of change
Festiniog in the Fifties
Festiniog in the Sixties
Isle of Wight Lines 50 years of change
Railways to Victory 1944-46
Return to Blaenau 1970-82
SECR Centenary album
Talyllyn 50 years of change
Yeovil 50 years of change

LONDON SUBURBAN RAILWAYS

Caterham and Tattenham Corner
Charing Cross to Dartford
Clapham Jn. to Beckenham Jn.
Crystal Palace (HL) & Catford Loop
East London Line
Finsbury Park to Alexandra Palace
Kingston and Hounslow Loops
Lewisham to Dartford
Lines around Wimbledon
London Bridge to Addiscombe
Mitcham Junction Lines
North London Line
South London Line
West Croydon to Epsom
West London Line
Willesden Junction to Richmond
Wimbledon to Beckenham
Wimbledon to Epsom

STEAMING THROUGH

Steaming through Cornwall
Steaming through the Isle of Wight
Steaming through Kent
Steaming through West Hants
Steaming through West Sussex

TRAMWAY CLASSICS

Aldgate & Stepney Tramways
Barnet & Finchley Tramways
Bath Tramways
Brighton's Tramways
Bristol's Tramways
Burton & Ashby Tramways
Camberwell & W.Norwood Tramways
Clapham & Streatham Tramways
Croydon's Tramways

Dover's Tramways
East Ham & West Ham Tramways
Edgware and Willesden Tramways
Eltham & Woolwich Tramways
Embankment & Waterloo Tramways
Enfield & Wood Green Tramways
Exeter & Taunton Tramways
Greenwich & Dartford Tramways
Hammersmith & Hounslow Tramways
Hampstead & Highgate Tramways
Hastings Tramways
Holborn & Finsbury Tramways
Ilford & Barking Tramways
Kingston & Wimbledon Tramways
Lewisham & Catford Tramways
Liverpool Tramways 1. Eastern Routes
Liverpool Tramways 2. Southern Routes
Liverpool Tramways 3. Northern Routes
Maidstone & Chatham Tramways
Margate to Ramsgate
North Kent Tramways
Norwich Tramways
Portsmouth's Tramways
Reading Tramways
Seaton & Eastbourne Tramways
Shepherds Bush & Uxbridge Tramways
Southampton Tramways
Southend-on-sea Tramways
Southwark & Deptford Tramways
Stamford Hill Tramways
Twickenham & Kingston Tramways
Victoria & Lambeth Tramways
Waltham Cross & Edmonton Tramways
Walthamstow & Leyton Tramways
Wandsworth & Battersea Tramways

TROLLEYBUS CLASSICS

Bournemouth Trolleybuses
Croydon Trolleybuses
Derby Trolleybuses
Hastings Trolleybuses
Maidstone Trolleybuses
Portsmouth Trolleybuses
Reading Trolleybuses
Woolwich & Dartford Trolleybuses

WATERWAY ALBUMS

Kent and East Sussex Waterways
London to Portsmouth Waterways
West Sussex Waterways

MILITARY BOOKS

Battle over Portsmouth
Battle over Sussex 1940
Bombers over Sussex 1943-45
Bognor at War
Military Defence of West Sussex
Military Signals from the South Coast
Secret Sussex Resistance
Surrey Home Guard

OTHER RAILWAY BOOKS

Index to all Middleton Press stations
Industrial Railways of the South
South Eastern & Chatham Railway
London Chatham & Dover Railway
War on the Line (SR 1939-45)

BIOGRAPHIES

Garraway Father & Son
Mitchell & company